FIERCE NFL RIVALRIES
12 SUPER-CHARGED MATCHUPS

by Matt Scheff

12 STORY LIBRARY

www.12StoryLibrary.com

Copyright © 2016 by Peterson Publishing Company, North Mankato, MN 56003. All rights reserved. No part of this book may be reproduced or utilized in any form or by any means without written permission from the publisher.

12-Story Library is an imprint of Peterson Publishing Company and Press Room Editions.

Produced for 12-Story Library by Red Line Editorial

Photographs ©: Mike Roemer/AP Images, cover, 1, 5; Vernon Biever/AP Images, 4; Rusty Kennedy/AP Images, 6; Bill Kostroun/AP Images, 8; AP Images, 10; G. Newman Lowrance/AP Images, 11; Paul Kitagaki Jr./The Sacramento Bee/AP Images, 12, 29; Richard Lipski/AP Images, 15; Scott Boehm/AP Images, 16, 28; David Drapkin/AP Images, 17, 19; Charles Krupa/AP Images, 18; Al Golub/AP Images, 21; NFL Photos/AP Images, 22; John Bazemore/AP Images, 25; Greg Trott/AP Images, 26

ISBN
978-1-63235-152-4 (hardcover)
978-1-63235-192-0 (paperback)
978-1-62143-244-9 (hosted ebook)

Library of Congress Control Number: 2015934297

Printed in the United States of America
Mankato, MN
June, 2015

Go beyond the book. Get free, up-to-date content on this topic at 12StoryLibrary.com.

TABLE OF CONTENTS

BEARS AND PACKERS CLASH IN NFL'S OLDEST RIVALRY

Chicago and Green Bay. It's the oldest rivalry in the National Football League (NFL). The Bears and Packers have been butting heads since 1921. That was only the NFL's second season. The Bears were still known as the Chicago Staleys.

It's also a classic border battle. These cold-weather foes are just over 200 miles (322 km) apart. Both play in outdoor stadiums. Snow, wind, and bitter cold often play a role when they meet.

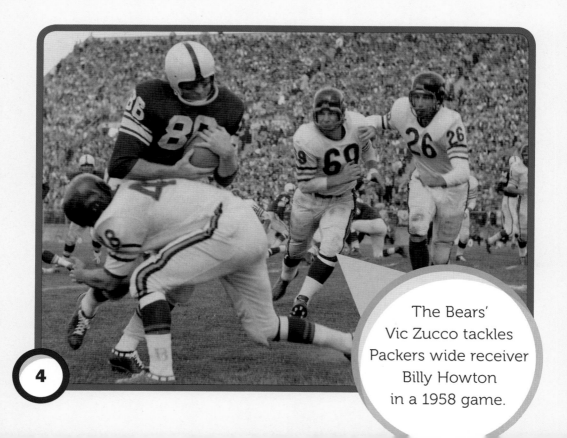

The Bears' Vic Zucco tackles Packers wide receiver Billy Howton in a 1958 game.

The bad blood between these teams started early. In 1924, Chicago's Frank Hanny and Green Bay's Tillie Voss got into a fight. They became the first players ever ejected for fighting. The Bears often beat the Packers in those early years. In 1941, the teams finished tied atop the NFL's West Division. It was playoff time. The Bears crushed the Packers 33–14.

The Packers took charge in the 1960s. Green Bay coach Vince Lombardi led the team to five NFL titles. Among those wins were the first two Super Bowls. The Packers went 15–5 against the Bears during that decade.

The teams met again after the 2010 season. It was their first playoff meeting in almost 70 years. Green Bay quarterback Aaron Rodgers took charge. The Packers surged to a 21–14 win. That sent them to the Super Bowl.

190

Games between the Bears and Packers through 2014, including playoffs.

- Chicago leads the all-time series 93–91–6, including playoffs.
- The 2010 playoffs marked only the fourth time that both teams were in the postseason together.
- The teams did not meet in 1982. A players' strike shortened that NFL season.

The Packers' Clay Matthews (top) tackles the Bears' Matt Forte in a 2014 game.

RAVENS AND STEELERS BATTLE FOR THE NORTH

The Baltimore Ravens made their NFL debut in 1996. The Pittsburgh Steelers promptly beat them 31–17. A new rivalry was born. But in some ways, an old rivalry was just heating up.

The Ravens had been the Cleveland Browns. From 1950 to 1995, the Browns and Steelers were two of the NFL's biggest rivals. Then the Browns' owner made a shocking decision. He moved the team to

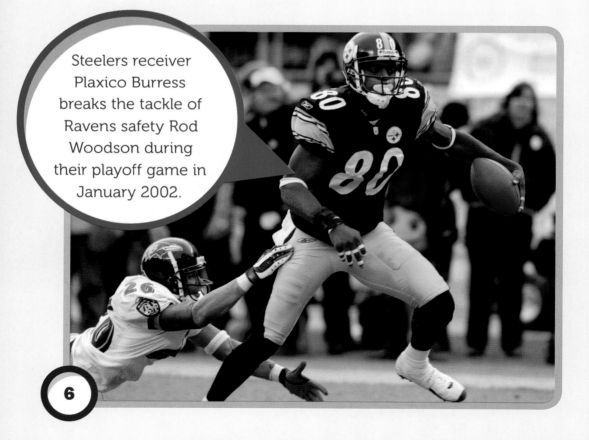

Steelers receiver Plaxico Burress breaks the tackle of Ravens safety Rod Woodson during their playoff game in January 2002.

Baltimore. That's when the team became the Ravens.

The new rivalry quickly got heated. Both teams often had tough defenses. And both teams usually won a lot of games. Their meetings often helped decide who won the American Football Conference (AFC) North Division. After the 2001 season, they faced off in the playoffs. Pittsburgh's defense dominated the game. Baltimore quarterback Elvis Grbac threw three interceptions. The Steelers won 27–10.

For the next decade, the teams remained among the NFL's best. Their biggest clash came in the AFC Championship Game following the 2008 season. Pittsburgh was clinging to a 16–14 lead late in the game. Baltimore was on the move. That's when Steelers safety Troy Polamalu picked off Baltimore quarterback Joe Flacco. Polamalu returned the interception 40 yards for the game-sealing touchdown. Pittsburgh went on to win the Super Bowl.

4

Playoff meetings between the Ravens and Steelers through 2014. Pittsburgh won three of four.

- The Ravens and Steelers have each won two Super Bowls in this century.
- The Ravens won after the 2000 and 2012 seasons.
- The Steelers won after the 2005 and 2008 seasons.

RETURN OF THE BROWNS

The Cleveland Browns returned to the NFL in 1999. The Browns haven't enjoyed much success since their return. But their old rivalry with the Steelers picked right back up. Browns fans also haven't forgotten that the Ravens' owner moved the original Browns. Luckily for fans, all three teams are in the AFC North. That means they play each other twice each year.

BAD BLOOD FLOWS BETWEEN PATRIOTS AND JETS

It hardly matters the sport. Fans in Boston and New York just seem to dislike each other.

That's certainly the case with the New England Patriots and New York Jets.

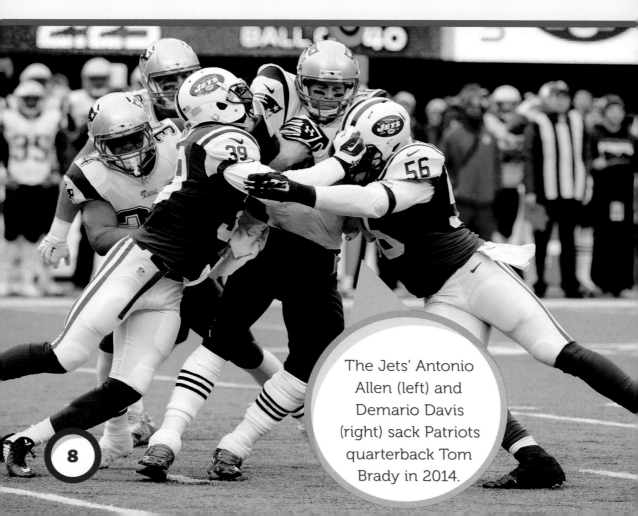

The Jets' Antonio Allen (left) and Demario Davis (right) sack Patriots quarterback Tom Brady in 2014.

Both teams began in 1960. They played in the upstart American Football League (AFL). Their first game was a thriller. The Boston Patriots beat the New York Titans 28–24. The Titans became the Jets in 1963. The Patriots became known as New England in 1971. That was one year after the AFL merged with the NFL.

The rivalry stepped up a notch in 1966. That year the teams met in the last game of the regular season. A brash young quarterback named Joe Namath led the Jets to victory. That denied the Patriots a division title. However, hard times fell on both clubs soon after.

Then, in 2000, Bill Belichick changed everything. He was a Jets assistant coach. When coach Bill Parcells

22–10

The Patriots' record against the Jets under Bill Belichick, through the 2014 season.

- The Jets and Patriots play in the AFC East Division.
- In 1998, the Jets signed star running back Curtis Martin away from the Patriots. Martin went on to become a hall of famer.

retired, Belichick was supposed to replace him. But Belichick instead took the head coaching job for New England. There, he and quarterback Tom Brady built perhaps the greatest NFL dynasty of the era. They won four Super Bowls from the 2001 through 2014 seasons.

WRITTEN ON A NAPKIN

In 2000, the Jets called a press conference to announce Bill Belichick as their new coach. At the press conference, Belichick wrote out his resignation on a napkin. He announced instead that he would coach the Patriots. A bitter legal battle followed. In the end, the Patriots gave the Jets several draft picks, and Belichick headed to New England.

9

4

CHIEFS AND RAIDERS CLASH OUT WEST

The Kansas City Chiefs and Oakland Raiders both began in the AFL. Neither had close neighbors. So they turned to each other.

The Chiefs and Raiders constantly battled for control of the AFL West. No game was bigger than their 1968 playoff. Each team finished 12–2. They met in a playoff to decide the division champ. The Raiders left no doubt, beating the Chiefs 41–6. A year later, the Chiefs got their revenge. They upset the Raiders to advance to the Super Bowl.

The Chiefs' Mike Garrett stiff-arms the Raiders' Rodger Bird in a 1967 game.

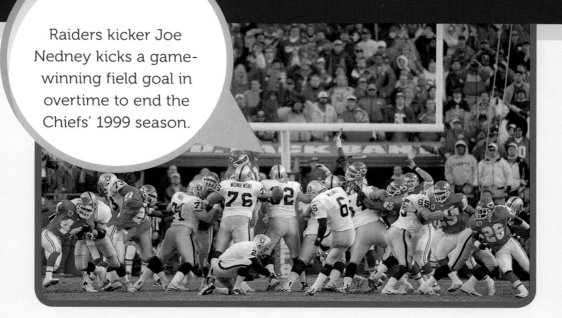

Raiders kicker Joe Nedney kicks a game-winning field goal in overtime to end the Chiefs' 1999 season.

The AFL merged with the NFL in 1970. The teams met for the first time in the NFL that year. Both benches cleared in a brawl. From there, the teams' fortunes took opposite paths. The Chiefs faded and became one of the league's worst teams. Meanwhile, the Raiders won three Super Bowls in the late 1970s and early 1980s.

The rivalry heated back up in the late 1990s. The teams played a series of exciting contests. One of the most memorable came in the final game of the 1999 regular season. The 9–6 Chiefs needed a win to get into the playoffs. Oakland, at 7–8, was just playing for pride. Yet the visiting Raiders crushed the hopes of Chiefs fans. Oakland kicker Joe Nedney booted a field goal in the final minute to tie the game at 38. Nedney then kicked another in overtime to end Kansas City's season.

20.5–19.3

All-time average score between the Chiefs and Raiders, with the Chiefs in the lead, through 2014.

- The Chiefs spent their first three seasons (1960–1962) as the Dallas Texans.
- From 1982 to 1994, the Raiders were located in Los Angeles.

SEAHAWKS AND 49ERS ARE NEW-SCHOOL FOES

Some rivalries escalate quickly. The Seattle Seahawks and San Francisco 49ers played in different divisions until 2002. One decade later, their games captivated fans all around the league.

The Seahawks hired Pete Carroll in 2010. The 49ers brought on Jim Harbaugh in 2011. The coaches had been rivals in college. They continued the tradition in the pros. Both built powerful teams. And both had similar strengths. Each had a smothering defense. Each had a multitalented quarterback, too. Colin Kaepernick led the 49ers. Russell Wilson starred for the Seahawks.

Tensions were high when the teams met late in 2012. Seattle shocked the 49ers with a 42–13 rout. Harbaugh was angry. He accused Seattle of cheating. The rivalry was really on. The teams met in one big game after another. The biggest was on January 19, 2014. The winner would move on to the Super Bowl.

The 49ers were marching late with a chance to win. That's when brash Seattle cornerback Richard Sherman stepped up. He tipped a pass in the end zone. Linebacker Malcolm Smith intercepted the pass, sealing the win. Seattle went on to win its first Super Bowl title.

6

Games played between the Seahawks and 49ers before 2002.

- The 49ers won four of those games.
- Pete Carroll won the battle of the coaches from 2011 to 2014. He went 5–4 against Jim Harbaugh.

The Seahawks' Richard Sherman tips a pass away from Michael Crabtree. The play sent Seattle to the Super Bowl after the 2013 season.

NO LOVE IS LOST BETWEEN DALLAS AND WASHINGTON

The Dallas Cowboys and Washington Redskins disliked each other before they even played a game. The Cowboys joined the NFL as an expansion team in 1960. Since they were brand new, they were allowed to pick players from current teams. Existing teams could protect some players. Washington quarterback Eddie LeBaron planned to retire. The team didn't protect him. But the Cowboys claimed him and convinced him to keep playing. Washington fans had their first reason to hate the Cowboys.

The relationship hasn't gotten any better since then. In 1979, the teams faced off in the final game of the season. The division title was on the line. Confident Washington players sent a funeral wreath to the Cowboys. It was their way of telling the Cowboys that their dynasty of the 1970s was dead. On the field, it looked like they were right. Washington led 34–21. Approximately six minutes remained. That's when Dallas quarterback Roger Staubach proved his nickname. "Captain Comeback" led the Cowboys to two quick touchdowns and a shocking victory. After the game, Dallas defensive

2

Playoff meetings between Dallas and Washington, after the 1972 and 1982 seasons.

- Washington won both playoff games.
- The biggest blowout in the series history came in a 38–3 Dallas victory in 1993.

Washington's Alfred Morris pushes away from Cowboys safety Eric Frampton in the 2012 season finale.

end Harvey Martin stormed into the Washington locker room. He hurled the wreath at the Washington players.

The final game of the 2012 regular season came with the same stakes. The winner would be the division champ. The loser would miss the playoffs. The focus was all on the star quarterbacks, Dallas's Tony Romo and Washington rookie Robert Griffin III. Yet it was Washington running back Alfred Morris who grabbed the headlines. He rushed for 200 yards and three touchdowns to lead Washington to victory.

VIKINGS CROWD IN ON PACKER TERRITORY

From 1920 to 1960, Minnesota was part of Green Bay Packers country. The Packers were the closest NFL team. So most Minnesota football fans rooted for them. That all changed in 1961. The Minnesota Vikings joined the NFL. The border battle was on.

The Packers and Vikings both played outdoors. Games at Met Stadium in Minnesota and Lambeau Field in Green Bay were often frigid. The teams would play in snow, ice, and wind. The weather forced the teams to play tough, hard-nosed football. Both teams often had powerful defenses.

The Vikings moved indoors in 1982. Yet the rivalry remained as competitive as any in the NFL. In 1992, quarterback Brett Favre became the face of the Packers for the next 15 years. Yet in 2008, the Packers cut ties with the aging quarterback. A year later, he turned up in a place Green Bay fans least wanted to see him—Minnesota.

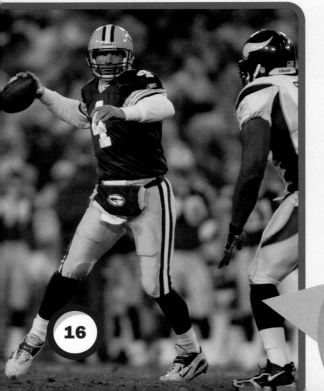

The Packers' Brett Favre passes against the Vikings in 2006.

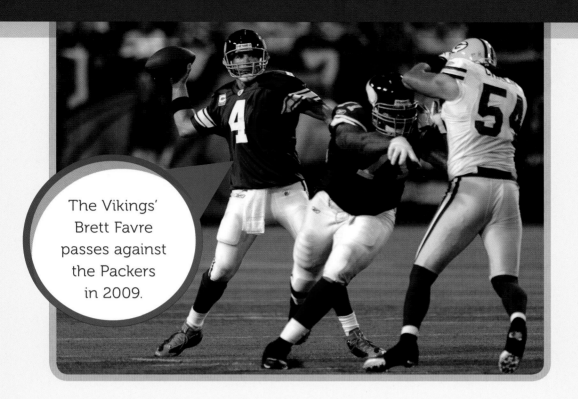

The Vikings' Brett Favre passes against the Packers in 2009.

Favre took it to his former team. He led the Vikings to two wins over the Packers that year.

The Packers got their revenge in the 2012 season. Minnesota beat Green Bay in the season's final game to qualify for the playoffs. But the Packers turned around and beat the Vikings in the playoffs' first round.

255

Games in which Brett Favre played for the Packers before joining the Vikings.

- From 1989 to 2004, either the Packers or Vikings won their division 11 of 16 times.
- The teams have met twice in the playoffs through 2014. Each team won a game.

THINK ABOUT IT

Packers fans spent years cheering for Brett Favre. How would you feel if you saw your favorite player wearing the uniform of one of your biggest rivals? Would you still root for that player?

SUPERSTAR PASSERS FUEL COLTS-PATRIOTS MATCHUPS

In the 2000s, few rivalries were as thrilling as the Indianapolis Colts versus the New England Patriots. To most football fans, a meeting between those teams boiled down to one thing: Peyton Manning versus Tom Brady.

The quarterbacks had very different backgrounds. Yet by the early 2000s, both were building legendary careers. They were the biggest stars in the NFL. Colts-Patriots games were must-watch television for NFL fans everywhere.

The Patriots' Tom Brady (12) and the Colts' Peyton Manning (18) after a January 2005 playoff game

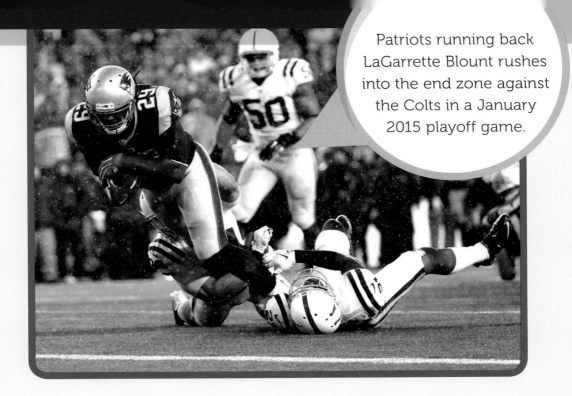

Patriots running back LaGarrette Blount rushes into the end zone against the Colts in a January 2015 playoff game.

The rivalry really began to take shape in 2003. The Patriots led a game 31–10. Then Manning led the Colts to a stunning comeback. The Patriots held on to win. New England then knocked the Colts out of the playoffs after the 2003 and 2004 seasons. Two seasons later, it was the Colts' turn. They beat the Patriots in the AFC title game to punch their ticket to the Super Bowl.

A new No. 1 pick, Andrew Luck, replaced Manning as the Colts' star passer in 2012. The rivalry was rekindled when the Patriots beat the Colts in the playoffs following the 2013 and 2014 seasons.

6

Combined NFL Most Valuable Player (MVP) Awards won by Peyton Manning and Tom Brady over an eight-year period from 2003 to 2010.

- The Colts and Patriots both played in the AFC East from 1970 to 2001.
- Yet their rivalry didn't really take off until after the Colts moved to the AFC South in 2002.

19

DENVER AND OAKLAND DON'T PRETEND TO LIKE EACH OTHER

The Denver Broncos and Oakland Raiders both began in 1960 as members of the AFL. They've played in the same division ever since. And the two teams built up some bad blood over the years.

Their rivalry really heated up in the late 1980s. Al Davis owned the Raiders. In 1988, he plucked up-and-coming coach Mike Shanahan from Denver's coaching staff. But Davis was known for being impatient and impulsive. And four games into Shanahan's second season, Davis fired him.

Shanahan took the firing personally. He still remembered it when he became the Broncos' coach six years later. Back in Denver, he made the Raiders enemy No. 1. The hatred wasn't one-way. Davis refused even to speak to his former employee.

The rivalry was at its peak in the 1990s. Both sides had competitive teams. They split their regular-season series 10–10 during the decade. However, the Raiders won their only playoff meeting in a 42–24 blowout. Shanahan and the Broncos got the last laugh, however. They won Super Bowls after the 1997 and 1998 seasons.

The rivalry has cooled somewhat in recent years. Shanahan was fired after the 2008 season, while

24
Points by which the Broncos led the Raiders at halftime in a 1988 game.

- The Raiders came back to win 30–27.
- Al Davis also coached the Raiders from 1963 to 1965.

Broncos running back Terrell Davis runs away from Raiders linebacker Rob Fredrickson in a 1997 game.

Davis died in 2011. Meanwhile, the Raiders went through a down period. Still, fans in both Denver and Oakland remember one of football's most bitter rivalries and wait for the day that it rises again.

THINK ABOUT IT

Rivalries form for many reasons. Which NFL rivalry is your favorite? What characteristics make that rivalry so exciting?

GIANTS AND EAGLES RIVALRY BUILT ON LONG HISTORY

The New York Giants and Philadelphia Eagles have been playing since 1933. And they've never liked each other one bit.

The dislike grew over the years. It hit a high in 1960. The teams were battling for the Eastern Division title. The Giants were driving, trailing by

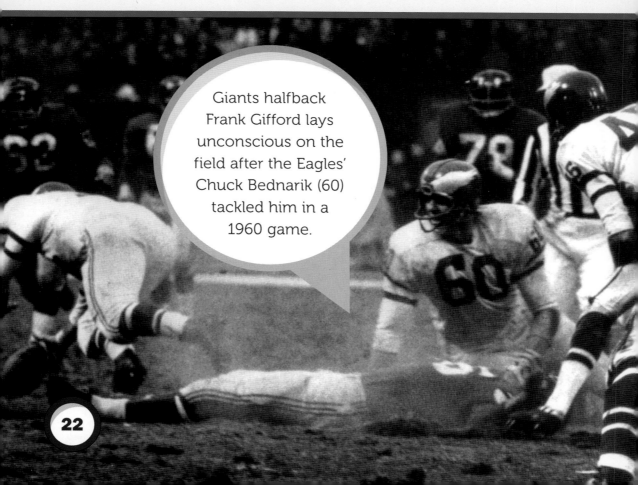

Giants halfback Frank Gifford lays unconscious on the field after the Eagles' Chuck Bednarik (60) tackled him in a 1960 game.

seven points. That's when halfback Frank Gifford caught a short pass. Gifford turned up the field. But Eagles linebacker Chuck Bednarik was there to meet him. Bednarik slammed into Gifford with a vicious

56

Points by which the Giants beat the Eagles in a shutout in their first meeting in 1933.

- New York and Philadelphia are separated by approximately 100 miles (161 km).
- The teams have met in the playoffs four times, with each team winning twice.

hit. Gifford lay unconscious on the field. He missed the rest of the season and all of 1961. The play became known as "The Hit."

The rivals gave fans another memorable game in 1978. The Giants led the Eagles 17–12. They held the ball with just 31 seconds remaining. Quarterback Joe Pisarcik took the snap and turned to hand off to fullback Larry Csonka. But they botched the handoff. The ball fell to the ground. The Eagles' Herman Edwards picked it up. Then he dashed all the way to the end zone for an unbelievable game-winning touchdown.

DEEP SOUTH PRIDE DEFINES FALCONS-SAINTS SERIES

The Deep South, also called Dixie, stretches from Louisiana to the Carolinas. It's a place where football passion runs high. For decades, fans in the Deep South had just two NFL teams: the Atlanta Falcons and the New Orleans Saints.

The Falcons and Saints first played in 1967. Fans and reporters called the game the Dixie Championship. The Saints earned bragging rights with a 27–24 victory. Neither team had much success in the decades after that, though. The rivalry cooled.

Finally, in the 2000s, both teams' fortunes took turns for the better. They became the dominant teams in the new National Football Conference (NFC) South. Fans eagerly awaited their high-scoring battles.

One of the biggest games came late in the 2010 season. The teams clashed on *Monday Night Football*. The division title up was for grabs. It was a rare defensive struggle. The Falcons' Chauncey Davis finally broke things open in the fourth quarter. He picked off a pass from Saints quarterback Drew Brees. Then he ran it all the way back for a touchdown. That put Atlanta up

2,019–1,890

All-time series score, in favor of the Saints.

- The Saints won the Super Bowl after the 2009 season.
- The Falcons reached the Super Bowl after the 1998 season but lost.

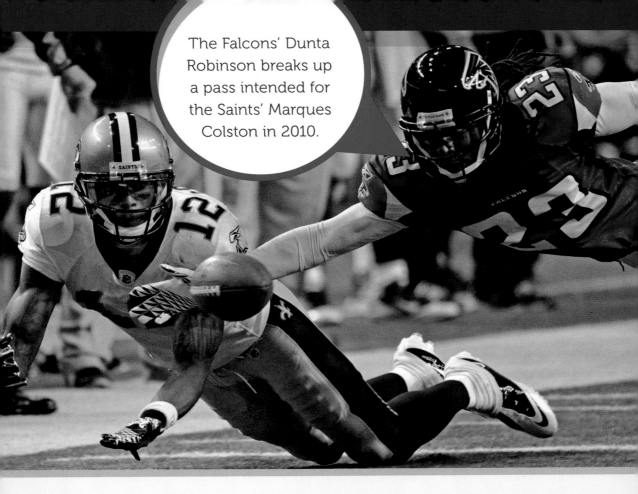

The Falcons' Dunta Robinson breaks up a pass intended for the Saints' Marques Colston in 2010.

14–10. But Brees and the Saints bounced back. He marched his team down the field. Then he zipped a touchdown pass to tight end Jimmy Graham to seal the 17–14 victory.

HURRICANE KATRINA

In August 2005, Hurricane Katrina devastated New Orleans. The home of the Saints, the Superdome, was badly damaged. The Saints were homeless for the entire 2005 season. They split their games between Baton Rouge, Louisiana, and San Antonio, Texas. The team's first game back in 2006 was a dramatic win over the Falcons.

DYNASTIES COLLIDE AS COWBOYS AND 49ERS CLASH

Many rivals are from nearby cities. Many play in the same division. That's not always the case, though. Sometimes heated rivalries spring up when two dominant teams seem to keep butting heads. That's what happened with the Dallas Cowboys and San Francisco 49ers.

49ers cornerback Deion Sanders intercepts a pass intended for Cowboys receiver Alvin Harper during a 1994 game.

The Cowboys were the dominant team in the NFC during the late 1970s. Quarterback Joe Montana and the 49ers took over in the 1981 season. The two teams met for the NFC title. Dallas was clinging to a late lead. That's when Montana led a last-ditch drive down the field. It ended with "The Catch." Receiver Dwight Clark leaped high into the air to snag the game-winning touchdown. San Francisco went on to win four Super Bowls in the 1980s.

Dallas and San Francisco kept going at it in the early 1990s. From the 1992 to 1994 seasons, they met in three straight NFC Championship Games. Troy Aikman, Emmitt Smith, and the Cowboys won two. Steve Young and the 49ers won one. The Cowboys won three Super Bowls in the 1990s, while the 49ers won one.

17-16-1

The 49ers' record in the all-time series with the Cowboys through 2014.

- Dallas, however, has won five of seven postseason contests.
- Cornerback Deion Sanders won a Super Bowl with San Francisco in 1994.
- Sanders won a Super Bowl with the Cowboys the next year.

THE STAR

One of the most memorable Cowboys-49ers moments came in 2000 in Dallas. San Francisco wide receiver Terrell Owens caught a touchdown pass. Then he ran to midfield to celebrate on Dallas's logo, a blue star. Later in the game he tried to do it again. This time Dallas defender George Teague put a stop to it. Teague laid out Owens with a huge hit, much to Cowboys fans' delight. Owens later played for the Cowboys from 2006 to 2008.

27

FUN FACTS AND STORIES

- In 1985, Green Bay Packers players dumped a load of horse manure in the Chicago Bears' locker room before a game. The prank probably didn't feel so funny when the Bears won the game 16–10 and went on to a Super Bowl title.

- The Indianapolis Colts and New England Patriots met in a regular-season game in 2009. The Patriots had a lead with just 2:08 to go. It was fourth down on their own 28-yard line. Most coaches would have punted. Bill Belichick had other ideas. He went for it. The huge gamble backfired. Tom Brady threw a pass to Kevin Faulk that came up a yard short. Peyton Manning and the Colts took over and easily marched to the winning touchdown.

- Talented Minnesota Vikings wide receiver Randy Moss was always a thorn in the Packers' side. That was never more true than when the team clashed in the playoffs following the 2004 season. Moss and the Vikings steamrolled the favored Packers. After one of his two touchdown catches, Moss pretended to pull down his pants and "moon" the Green Bay crowd.

- In 2013, Pittsburgh Steelers coach Mike Tomlin almost made a tackle against the Ravens. Baltimore's Jacoby Jones was returning a kick. Jones streaked down the sideline as Tomlin stuck his leg onto the field. The move earned Tomlin a $100,000 fine, but it also helped a defender make the tackle.

- Baseball helped fuel the rivalry between the Chiefs and Raiders. After the 1967 season, the Kansas City Athletics moved to Oakland. Two years later, the Kansas City Royals formed. Kansas City baseball fans never forgave the Athletics for moving, and that distaste carried over to Oakland's football team.

GLOSSARY

brawl
A rough, disorderly fight.

dominate
To take command or control over something.

dynasty
A long-lasting period of dominance for a team or player.

expansion team
A brand-new team added to an existing league.

merged
When two groups combine to make one.

resignation
To give up one's job.

rookie
A first-year player.

shutout
When one team is unable to score in a game.

strike
When employees refuse to work as a form of protest.

unconscious
A state of not being awake that is often caused by an injury to the head.

upset
A victory by a team expected by most to lose.

FOR MORE INFORMATION

Books

Doeden, Matt. *Outrageous Football Rivalries*. North Mankato, MN: Capstone Press, 2015.

Lee, Tony. *Greatest Rivalries in Sports*. Minneapolis, MN: Abdo Publishing, 2013.

Rausch, David. *National Football League*. Minneapolis, MN: Bellwether Media, 2014.

Websites

NFL Rush
www.nflrush.com

Pro Football Hall of Fame
www.profootballhof.com

Pro Football Reference
www.pro-football-reference.com

Sports Illustrated Kids
www.sikids.com

INDEX

About the Author

Matt Scheff is an artist and author living in Alaska. He enjoys mountain climbing, deep-sea fishing, and curling up with his two Siberian huskies to watch football.

READ MORE FROM 12-STORY LIBRARY

Every 12-Story Library book is available in many formats, including Amazon Kindle and Apple iBooks. For more information, visit your device's store or 12StoryLibrary.com.